DICKON HAPPER

Sonnets For Dogs And Cats

Published by Future Poetry Library

an imprint of JonesCat Publishing Ltd

Edinburgh

www.jonescat.com

ISBN 978-1-9999204-6-3

Printed and bound in Great Britain by Bell and Bain Ltd, Glasgow

For Benny, Sam, Orlando, Caval, Kate, Holly, Rusty, Midge, Judy, Old Tom (Moth-eater), Harry, Pip, Shmoo, Jonesy, Floyd and JJ.

I love you all and always will.

CONTENTS

DOGS

CATS

DOGS AND CATS

DOGS

Be careful, now, and keep your tail in mind

Be careful, now, and keep your tail in mind
You oft forget that it belongs to you
Despite it being secured to your behind
No afterthought is it but dogness true.
Remember, then, the wine glass on the stool
The mess it made when in a flash destemmed
More precious though your own red-blooded pool
Mere crystal's cheap; your fright may never mend.
For when the world is sad that dog has passed
Here comes a fine and wagging exclamation
An extra bit of him that flies at last
A crescendo and finale and ovation -
Our tail to us is an unworthy story
Yet is to others our defining glory.

We chanced upon a handsome greyhound pair

We chanced upon a handsome greyhound pair
You pranced in falling leaves and sped around
I danced sure words with owner equally fair
By hazel copse we both were making ground.
When sudden broke two deer; in sharp surprise
they fled; the greyhounds' eyes sharp glistened clear
Then as smoke before a hurricane they atomised
To coalesce a hundred yards from here.
You stood without a hope your play cut dead
You didn't even try to chase - you knew
This was a different game with rules unread
But take no shame in such a trouncing true
They too will be outrun one autumn day
By a toothless limping dog with muzzle grey.

V

The V.E.T. - the dreaded acronym
Not needed, for you sense it from my face
I have to nod: we're going to that place
Your body folds, your eyes with silver brim
Betrayal! Am I not the magic hound
Who fishes treats from pockets, who stands tall
Who whisks you to the beach, can throw a ball
finds food each night and drives the car around?
Could I not make a simple pain recede?
No, my pet, I cannot. And go we must.
Your horror at my flaying of our trust
Reminds me of another ruthless deed
A love who one day came to kill not kiss
And though I wept she did not flinch or miss.

E

A purgatory, doom of cowering beasts
Interred alive in coffins with a view
The torture chamber soon their sole release
"The vet will see you now. It's time - go through."
The green light in the hall revealing fears
In me as much as you - your liquid eyes
Destroy my will, untap my burning tears
Too loud my gunshot heartbeat amplifies.
"What seems to be amiss?" so clear and still
her voice it lifts me just enough to groan:
"It's very hard to say. My pet is ill
In truth? I worry I will die alone."
Did I say that?! My soul is bare to see!
A smile - a hope: "You both look good to me."

T

Sure fingers plunge through fur jab hard in ways
I would not dare. Black jowls pulled back beneath
Shine sharp wet mountain rows of death wolf teeth
No snarls or nips today: "Good boy," she says.
Four paw print damps on steel the only sign
Your bravery is feigned. Will pretty lips
deliver ugly facts? My heartbeart skips…
"This jab, some pills then bed and he'll be fine."
The door flies wide. I pay the bill. We're free
As dandelion seeds upon the breeze
The lost souls waiting envy our release
Her panacea smile is all I see.
You're better. Your distress is at an end
Now I am sick. I hope I never mend.

I showed you Venus, Jupiter and Mars

I showed you Venus, Jupiter and Mars
I told you of their seasons, speeds, their spins
They sparkle not and are not classed as stars
I ranked their orbits and aphelions.
Our rocky sister's shrouds are poison gas
Fat Jove can gulp the Earth a thousand times
The largest mountain ever Nergal has
No Life has risen from their frozen slimes.
You heard my words but then above the trees
She rose - the Moon - and you knew everything
She blessed your eyes and in her silver ease
You breathed and from your soul began to sing
You sang my heart across the endless night
My one and true eternal satellite.

I saw an ancient hound in Val d'Isère

I saw an ancient hound in Val d'Isère
As white and woolly as the tumbling snow
I had to smile at the resemblance there
Although it made me miss your presence so.
I hurried past - the ice then stole my feet
Sure, stiff and slow the old dog made a turn
And padded to my body in the street
Soft wearing like a garland his concern.
In wet and deep brown eyes I saw your grace
Though you lie far beyond the glacier peaks
He licked and knew at once my hurting face
In strange compassion your heart ever speaks.
The love you gave to me itself reflects
Returning love that more love then collects.

Damp dawn, we glimpsed a ghost dog you and I

Damp dawn, we glimpsed a ghost dog you and I
By fields edge, cantering under the yews
the mist within, a streak against the sky
Soft ears swept back, flecked with mud, confused
I'd seen him first when I was just a child
Encircling the haunts of his departed soul
As free as wind: lad masterless and wild
No 'Come!' to flee nor lead to keep him close
Pale envy'd kissed me, soft as April leaf
But all is different at this end of days
Black pity chills me, wet as mother's grief
To see him run old paths in ghostly haze
I shiver, recoiling from habitual ease
And lead us out beyond the sheltered trees.

A-hunting golf balls, finding thwarted dreams

A-hunting golf balls, finding thwarted dreams
One here, two there, unearthing ever more
Sharp gorse draws blood - be brave and treasure teems
We plunge on deeper to the bramble core.
My pockets brim with hopes that high once flew
For every one a player stood on tee
Envisioning a smite to split the blue
A swing one atom out - black misery!
Stop now - some lie so deep they'll ne'er be found
Let's home, to daub these orbs with marker pen
My name will change their luck this time around
Tomorrow they'll fly true for me, and then-
Oh, silly dog! each ball you find you bite
Hold gently on these brilliant spheres of white.

With every sleepy dawn the postman walks

With every sleepy dawn the postman walks
You know his shape, his face and voice, his gait
Warm smiles he gives you thank with savage barks
If Satan toted post you'd have no greater hate.
Why violence? What wrong has he done you?
Refrain, I beg! I seek delivery
Of letter rare - if too much ire you spew
he'll hedge it deep and inconvenience me!
But this your nature be - I should give thanks
How can I know an ever-smiling man
For whom I'm lost in even-numbered ranks?
When I to you am the beloved One?
It's not in strangers that life's danger lies
But those who close with no need of disguise.

Sky grey and wet as underside of corpse

Sky grey and wet as underside of corpse
snow blown into a telescope of trees
a view to naught for sightless eyes, iced hopes
as daylight cuts its own cold throat more keen
each turn of earth, and lower downs the sun
the solstice nears but dreams recede and ill
a paradox deep grows in me. Undone
I simply cannot see the light. No will
to stay the flood of final lethargy
the snow bank calls, my anvil feet travail -
you whine. I'm stopped by sight of what will be:
you running masterless in winter hail…
No end that starts such pain is worthy rest
Today, I stay. With you. For worst. For best.

We found the first sweet daffodil of spring

We found the first sweet daffodil of spring
Black winter'd sprawled across the world too long
Corrupt and rank, an old and rotten king
One yellow bloom began again my song-
-you ate it! One brief sniff and smiling bite
jowls tumbling petalled drops of molten gold
How could you? Kill pure beauty at first sight
A bomb-struck dam's flood water drowned me cold.
A life of mine that died as it was born
Expected smiles extinguished into sighs
A bursting bloom that I will ever mourn…
…I stayed my fist before your guileless eyes.
My child! You only saw the honeyed flower.
You tasted spring so we can live this hour.

The guide dog who failed

A furry blur sprayed dirt and stole your stick
You stared - affronted by this cheeky trick
The owner calmly said, "Now Benny, stop,"
A canine shrug - the booty duly dropped
right by your paws. "So well-behaved!" I cried.
"A guide dog trained he is," the man replied.
"At first assigned a blind old gent in town.
That job he failed - he just kept sitting down."
"To wait for cars to pass? Or kids on bikes?
It must be wearing watching all the time."
A rueful shake: "He just sits when he likes.
So now our walks can follow no design
And unexpected corners of the world
Are blazing banners quietly unfurled."

The woods are always perfect

This elm you sent rude squirrels up to flee
And planted paws to bark at bouncing tails
(Its rippled trunk a cheat code in 3D)
Has toppled, breathed aside by April gales.
Path blocked we walk where brambles hold few smells
And views are less of leaves and more of town
Perhaps these folded steps and secret spells
Will grow to hold the old way's proud renown.
I rue the change. And yet the wood is true
Each day a corner dies, soft life rots through
While fresh-lit mossy shadows breathe anew
Twas thus the day we came; tomorrow too
Into the woods we two again must go
Forever pure yet never found just-so.

Who's most surprised, the rabbit, me or you

Who's most surprised, the rabbit, me or you
As gorse explodes and there you stand jaws stuffed
A pet transformed: your hunting hound debut
Brute instinct fires; you shake it hard enough
To crack soft bones (the deepest kiss of all)
It flies and crumples - can I save its neck?
I gallop, bend, but cannot fate forestall
Poor rabbit. Gone with no chance to object.
A pause - you lay as one in mourning sense
Then filled an oath made by your sires untamed
And ate as hunger trained them ages hence
In love and death the game's rules are the same
The battle loser finds their calling true
The winner wears old colours cast anew.

This puppy is an idiot

This puppy is an idiot you say
Dismissing goofy paw pats with a sneer
May I remind you 'twas less than a year
Since bounding up you went in just that way.
To every dog you saw you'd prance around
Tongue lolling, knowing not the protocol
They cut you dead; if noticed you at all
In schoolyard tears are friendships drowned.
How quick we age and think ourselves so wise
And reach the stage our own youth chills our hearts
While even as our elders us despise
It never ends; at least, my child, it starts -
When we learn why our pain arrived (and how)
We love the hurt that others hold right now.

The dead tree scrolls

A blazing column, pollen dancing gold
arrests my vagabond steps; a canopy door
unfilled by sycamore umbra, leases bold
azure soft foothold on the forest floor.
Spotlit I stand in paparazzi motes,
a bone-white trunk shocked limbless, huge, bark-nude
commands my eyes on high to secret holes
not nests or dreys: there paper notes extrude.
(Your rustles fade; lost hunt pursues old breath.)
Time stops. The writer? Reader? When? Why there?
My questions dance more than the gilded air
Perhaps the tree has scripted its own death
My vow to bring a ladder is no good
Forgotten by the time I leave the wood.

The rain-walkers

Late spring had slunk from sun to gloom. The air
held seas, each blade of grass a brimming vat
of disappointed dew, but still we pair
walked our hopes. Clinging fur, sopping hat.
Hot optimism draws a weekly meet
Your tail-wag family, siblings, dam and sire
At friending owners I admit defeat;
Your bounding joy my limitless desire.
Tonight none came, our presence not enough
to light them through the rain; you looked so lost:
a child whose birthday party was rebuffed,
ghost invites drifting in the lonely mist.
You snorted, found a stick, forget those fools!
The park's all ours: still, silent, lit by jewels.

The only stick is one another holds

I pluck a birch branch from the forest floor
You want it more than miser wants his gold
You growl; I give; you drop it - now a bore.
The only stick is one another holds.
I scoff at fickle twists of canine mind
But now I wish I'd walked another way
And gone along the chuckling river side
Where we could toss and fetch in better play.
Brute envy is the engine powering all
Fat squirrel bored of every nut he's tried
No sooner triumph won than it feels small
The robin with new song dissatisfied.
This sonnet started well but now it's done
Read on, there's sure to be a better one.

Clatterpaws

"Tell us, mum, of silly Clatterpaws,"
Soft sleepy cubs abed in burrows said,
"the hopeless hunting hound with crashing tread
And breath so foul, 'tis ease to dodge his jaws!"
"Don't mock him, dears," Ma warned her feisty flock,
"you tease the storm. Beware of being proud;
The day you cannot hear for crowing loud
Wild luck will kiss his paws; he'll thunder not."
"Fie mother, we'll e'er hear his dopey feet
For we are smart and young and swift and- oh
My brother, dear, where did our mama go?"
"I don't know sis, there was a shadow fleet-"
"Then what? Oh silly boy, don't play the cheat!
Why, I'm not feared of Clatterpaws, you kn- ."

Have you been a good dog?

You look confused; no moral blame you see.
I check myself, was what you did a sin?
Wet eyes insist your act had good therein:
now we must weigh canine philosophy.
For Hume pure passion moves the paws to deed
Free will is Sartres' wild morality
While Kant's true reason rules dogality
Of higher good old Nietzsche sniffs no need.
Objectively you ate a tray of buns -
your paws upon the bench, your nose all crumbs,
and yet I'm with the Bard: you're good all through:
No man or dog to falseness e'er succumbs
if always to thine own self one is true
and stealing cakes is really very you.

I trust you're cooking sausages?

You moved! I trust you're cooking sausages?
I'll chum you up the hallway, if you please
At all things meat I really am a whizz.
I can give tips; advise on quantities.
Your first mistake - the kettle we don't need
The frying pan is just the man, take care
and get him out. Just tea this time - no feed?
Your eyes are good? You see the fridge right there?!
You're sitting down again. I will rest too.
You're right. Resist those brutish urge displays
And yet I hear your stomach call anew
When in such troubled, victual-less dark days-
Who isn't hungry, just a tad, that is?
You moved! I trust you're cooking sausages?

Chill autumn walking woods in russet time

Chill autumn walking woods in russet time
By crumbling castle walls and mossy oak
Owls soothe me, scent of childhood fires sublime
My senses overload - the mists de-cloak
True Mary, Queen of Scots! - her flag unfurls
Brisk pages trot and sneering lords surround
My mind, a sycamore samara, whirls
My tongue is lead; her pretty head gold-crowned.
You spy the spaniel trembling in her skirts
A wag, a wuff, you play to common rules
The regal toy's in awe of you! - she flirts
Moll smiles: "Are manners aught but maille for fools?"
No line of hist'ry will e'er be writ of me
The royallest dog on earth would bow to thee.

Thick snow, we lost a trail on Hogmanay

Nose gimballed microns o'er the crusted white
Furred shoulders rolling as a winter swell
You plough through briar, branch and burn sharp-iced
Surrendering all self to quarry's spell.
Glee-rosy you tow me light in step and heart
Towards a later treasure of my own:
Across the dark old friends come to my hearth
to celebrate a year both dead and born.
Hard halt! your paw it shakes, head sways with loss
One snowflake had its scent, the next did not.
Just as text tolls: "we cannot come tonight".
There's nothing now will draw us to the light.
Come by, we'll circle round the fields once more
Together, but - this time a little slower.

My boy, they're nigh immortal, by our days

My boy, they're nigh immortal, by our days
My master played in these same dunes with my
Ancestral sire five centuries gone by.
They're constant as our generations fade.
For almost my whole life he did not change
Just recently I saw his grey arrive
His dreams seem cruel; he lacks the will to strive
To see a god slow-falter moves me strange.
Of all his hounds, the ultimate am I
He knows it and will gift you to his son
Your life he'll be; you'll die when he's still young
Your great grand-pups will by his bedside lie.
So rare it is for one of them to pass
I only hope I guard him at the last.

CATS

I like to think you were a refugee

I like to think you were a refugee
Last time around life's ever-rolling wheel
Not for a wish of suffering in me
But for a sort of justice to be real.
False prisoner in dark yet living tomb
A beaten orphan begging in the rain
Now with each lick you soft and sweetly groom
You wash away a year of filth and pain.
To balance rank oppression now your soul
Can soothe itself all day upon my bed
Your body's plump; all wishes met unsaid
A bagatelle at last bounced to its hole.
Or was it I who hurt? Is this my fate?
And you're my salve, my solace incarnate.

I'm sorry, puss, am I disturbing you?

I'm sorry, puss, am I disturbing you?
Though I must get along (I'm running late)
I see you've lots of sleeping on your plate
May I suggest a plan to help you through?
Lie in, relax, don't start your work too soon
Pace yourself right and you'll have time to nap
At ten - and twelve - if there is no mishap
The serious kips you'll do this afternoon.
A yawn! A pro, you're doing well I see
And yes, a siesta first is only right
With all that grind you'll need an early night.
Forgive my digs, it's only jealousy:
My plans! I never achieved any of those
One tenth as well as sleepy cats can doze.

Sit on my lap - another will make the tea

Sit on my lap - another will make the tea
"I'm sorry, love, but look who's now at peace?
A shame 'twould be to crack her sweet release
So milk, two lumps, a bourbon cream for me."
I am becatted;

      no wind   no wave   no tide
can move my bones.

        My time is not my own
I serve; I am

       her warmth   her bed   her throne
When I move next

       cat captain will decide.
And for my patience she will grant me grace
Full calm - who cares that tea is not disbursed?
She roots herself and me within the universe
Creating unbound time, pure love-filled space.
No battle, work or human heart I've found
Gives wisdom more than sitting still, cat-bound.

A heaven for cats needs must be rife with mice

A heaven for cats needs must be rife with mice;
But mouse would see no cat in his rapture.
A paradox that makes me feel unsure;
Would I be part of your sweet paradise?
As you would surely star amid my bliss
I once thought all my felines past would gather
Around me joyful in the hereafter;
Until I minded grumpy feral Chris.
Hard life had he before dad's rescue care
He scratched, scarred and hated little me.
No purring could he make, nor laps could bear
A house alone: his eternity.
No soul can I compel to hold me fond
My love must love itself. Here and beyond.

Another midnight, another half-dead mouse

Another midnight, another half-dead mouse
by muffled thump and scurry I'm hauled from sleep
as deep as a womb. I stagger, draped in dreams
Dumb drowsy god, the titan of the house
Must stumble in a silly chase and keep
with cat, ignoring tiny rodent screams.
If more alive, salvation has a cost:
my soft return to peace and slumb'ring bed.
A quick dispatch with hefted boot is best
Pure violence will ruffle less my head.
But heavy sins will bruise while unconfessed
And sleep abuts the kingdom of the dead.
Glib execution's no exalted right
Avenging cthulhu mice will stalk my night.

If I could golf as well as you can hunt

If I could golf as well as you can hunt
I'd rise at dawn and tee off every day
My swing as smooth as your outrageous stunt
Of plucking unseen bats from deep inside
The blackest night, and rabbits twice your size
From holes, dispatching them without delay.
My drives would bound a fairway long and sit
Up ready for my wand to cast its spell,
Mere McIlroy would swoon and clutch his heart
At putts and chips with butter sweetness hit.
Or would my brilliance lose its gleam? Pure art
Outshining all must blind itself as well:
Sublimes pass in a flashing second flown
My unknown adequacy's set in stone.

How can it be? You liked this food last week

How can it be? You liked this food last week
You curled your tail and leaned and purred
Rejoice! I walked on air! At last I'd found
The grail - the holy meat of taste renowned
So then by rain and traffic undeterred
I drove for miles and queued, that brand to seek.
And now! Recoiling from the bowl you grouse
As if I'd served you filth unfit for swine
Your whimsy detonates my careful plans
Oh puss! I've purchased 96 big cans
It's hard to tell just where you draw the line
Last week you ate the rear end of a mouse.
You live, you eat: both à la carte
Which is for others an exhausting art.

Miaowing now is no real help at all

Miaowing now is no real help at all
The washer's flooded out the kitchen floor
Its trap is clogged with fur - a knotted ball
Your tubby belly can wait ten minutes more.
D'you know how many jobs are on my list?
Five bills need paid; a china horse wants glue;
A sliding drawer is stuck; the post I missed;
The parcel I awaited? Missed that too.
The clean and dirty clothes are in one pile;
I have the bank to call; a tyre is flat;
A lazy teen has left the toilet vile;
And now I'm nagged by a miaowing cat!
I yield: here, have your meat - at least that's done
I'm always others' errand number one.

Kurtz the cat

A tail, wet trail, fresh spoor of corpses raw
I track up-country, deep-piled jungle rug,
Mouse bodies scattered by your carmine paw
Amid them the destroyer god sits smug.
Mere hours ago you purred upon my knee,
Your paws soft pads, angelic fur-gilt mitts,
Sweet peace you gave, like dough you kneaded me,
But now your gnomon shadow Death befits.
Is blood your yang to yin of giving love?
Or only so much comfort can you bear
'Fore dagger claws must slide from gentle glove
And sleekit midnight welcomes home her slayer.
You've shown me plain your heart of darkness now
The horror, puss! Apocalypse miaow.

I dreamt of one long dead
who lived once more

I dreamt of one long dead who lived once more
In summer snapshot swimming by the weir
The tomboy playmate cousin I adored
Our smiles the ripples on the pool so clear.
The dream drove out foul memory - with cause
her plastic flesh pale-wasted and defiled
her adult bones hard-seized by giant claws
And crumpled in the coffin of a child.
I surface, groggy, wrecked at loss rewoken
You're on my bed - I smear away hot streams
Ashamed in pain - you smile these words unspoken:
"I am the cat who sleeps to share your dreams.
Like all we love your cousin she lives still
And while I sleep for you she always will."

We are the cats of the Colosseum

Rome's May sun roasts the sky with napalm flame
I wilt, scarce shaded by two thousand years
Of vaulted dark, where warriors of fame
made peace with death and smeared away love's tears.
In dust, a gang of tumbling sibling cats
Cavorts in beams and sports with downy mice
where lions slashed the blood from Christian throats
And dogs ripped kings apart for added spice.
I see a frantic lioness beg Fate:
"Preserve my cubs so young, I thee implore!
No spears to dodge or brutal men to hate."
"The price: they must remain here evermore."
For them we'd shrink the world to blunt its hurt
And build a circus in the sunny dirt.

I wonder how you'd like the île de Ré

I wonder how you'd like the île de Ré
The sleepy clinking boats, the sun-bright quay
A man and cat on summer holiday -
My current blessing would now double be!
We first explore Napoleonic walls
Then cycle cross the isle (up front you get!)
A café pause, then browse the market stalls
Before we *manger une ou deux crevettes.*
Why waste the Now with idle future dreams?
All things I like about here you'd detest
The waves, the salt, the wind, the noisy scenes
And that's not why our home life is the best
Just as our tastes diverge beyond compare
More precious are the tiny joys we share.

The cat who went to nursery

At my boy's nursery a cat strode in
A friendly tubby fellow, ginger furred
Delight like April sunshine blazed from him
A dozen children rubbed his tum - he purred.
"This cat is lost!" - the adults scanned his chip -
"He lives in Leeds, two hundred miles the trip!"
A stowaway on a removal van
(Oh puss, yours was a well-considered plan!)
And best of all they sent him back by train
First class - he munched on prawns and watched the rain.
That roving, rambling cat is now long gone
And totty grubby boys are six feet tall
But puss's grand adventure still lives on
Inside their smiles, in me, and with you all.

You miss nothing in the moment

Lost sunny nooks, the sleepy jade-green grass
High sentry fence where you'd command the street
The secret ferns, by fur pressed smooth as glass
Dark voids behind the shed with mice so sweet!
Unwarned we dropped you in an oubliette
Deleted this whole world and shipped you blind
As influential as a dinner set
By rights pure rage should overwhelm your mind
But here you purr. And instantly set out
On foot patrol to claim and mark new bounds
Exploring this strange realm as our brave scout,
Surrendered thoughts to feelings, sights, and sounds
No backwards glance or tears for time that's done
Just being here. At home. Right now. As one.

The inside cat and the outside cat

"O wild cat at my window, tell me of the world
your trails across yon infinite estate,
the canyons 'tween the sheds, the dashing birds
the jungle shrubberies, the scents of mates."
"Fine cat behind this glass, I will - but first
please sing of laps as soft and grand as thrones,
your bowl of treats and milk to slake your thirst
that pillow by the fire all your own."
"My treasures rich your will would suffocate.
Has nature lost its elemental spell?"
"The sharp wind keens my envy much of late
I'm drawn here as a nomad to a well."
"That's why I crave these briefest views of you,
For when you leave, my life I love anew."

Our sitter sends me pics of you reclined

Our sitter sends me pics of you reclined
Ecstatic: curling, splaying belly white.
Relief swabs guilt at leaving you behind
All's well; I stretch my bones by poolside bright.
Until a chill electrifies my spine:
Perhaps you're happier now I'm not there?
Your gift of intimacy's his not mine:
These pixels are a self-confessed affair.
Cool lemonade once sweet now warms and sours
and my return I dread; you'll huff to say
'Twas really I betrayed the trust once ours
And turn your back upon me for a day.
Oh clever cat: you act, I heed the call;
You've come with me on this trip after all.

Fossilised

I found myself on shaded, ancient street
Haze-stilled by summer, missed by tourist feet
My rosy childhood rolling like a ball
Down dusty gutters, bounce off crumbling walls
A corner kerb, the paving patched with grey
with pawprints flouncing 'cross the set cement
Just as they were a forty-year-gone day
And for my dad in his quick element.
But can that be the case? The paving's new
The concrete patch fresh-laid then must be too
So in the hours before it set awhile
A younger cat laid tracks, aloof, carefree?
The cat's the same. I recognise his style
Same street. Same me. It simply has to be.

Hordes

It started with a well-intended act
The fleeting kind that's girded your whole life
A stray and soaking imp more hedge than cat
You homed to care, but uncorked only strife;
Like all your woes, it multiplied when nursed
alone. And as before you locked me out.
Years passed, you drowned; but never owned your curse
Souls seventy-two you had when I turned rat.
You said I broke your heart - self-serving lie!
I saw the filth and twisted bones, eyes blown
Like soldiers in the lines, betrayed on high
Sick generations foul and famished grown
You loved them all, no doubt; but, yes, I blame
Your use of beauty born to hide your shame.

You mourn the kittens who can never be

Still Sunday hours, you sit contently
Scuffed boards, white lily, dust, the window bay
A cloud will pass and shadow cast you grey
And in that moment I see memory
descend on you just as it falls on me
(so black sometimes I hear the devil pray)
I know your mind, though you've no power to say:
You mourn the kittens who can never be.
A tear or two, who cares or gives a damn?
My dream of futures lost before they're found
Brief wond'ring, wand'ring freedom of the mind
The who they would have been and who I am
The questions asked, the answers silent bound
Our own lost golden chances to be kind.

There is a bad cat in the neighbourhood

"Beware," an old dear told me o'er the wall,
"There is a bad cat in the neighbourhood
It stalks the dusky fences, plots no good
And battered Muffin for no slight at all.
The dog at 47's stiff with fright,
it Kruegerises mammals by my door
to send a bloody message. Pray watch for
its crooked tail and eyes of demon light."
"I'll stay alert for evil claws," I said;
inside I grinned with pride - that cat of sin
is purring on my bed; its deadly paw
dark represents a will in me un-met:
To show outside this latte-drinking skin
A soul that others talk about with awe.

I give my cat her annual performance review

For grooming, sleeping, yoga - all grade A
A-plus for looking regal's only fair
Another A for giving walls a stare
And begging food? Distinction I must say.
But mousing it's D minus as your mark
Your hunting has a single success lacked
Is there a cat-mice non-aggression pact?
Or other reason for this lack of spark?
I trust you'll vow to boost this score…
Your flashing eyes - you cannot bear defeat -
and now I see who's judging whom the more
the scores you had for me are plunging lower.
Again I've failed the year: your marks downbeat
ah well. It's one I'm happy to repeat.

The tiny choices of others

Past morns you'd slumber on the laundry pile,
of late you've picked a new spot in the hall
to curl, your nose a whisker from the wall;
strange sorrow holds me at your change in style.
I smiled to see you as I fussed my day,
defiant sloth - your habits my hope found
at least someone was living life unbound;
your choices landmarks pointing custom's way.
If illness made you move I could admit
the shift; but no, you roved for cause unknown;
what right have I to set your whims in stone?
My only life surrendered ownership:
soul's will is weak if all my acts pre-writ
defined by tiny choices not my own.

The next kitten

"Of course no kitten can replace old puss
But here we have a chance to love once more
A personality so fresh and loose
We'll shape its world and teach it to adore."
I said all that and meant it long days past
You smiled and we did then what I thought wise
But now all I beheld is gone at last:
his tiny kitten paws. Your shining eyes.
If we could buy new humans to succeed
Would I browse flotsam in the rescue home
or cold-select a breeder's pedigree?
High-priced the soul to leave me less alone:
a kitten's both an ending and a start
as every smile can one day pierce your heart.

"Why is your cat so fat?" the wee girl cried

"Why is your cat so fat?" the wee girl cried.
"And never seems to sit with us at all?"
Her grandpa smiled, "My dear, he roams so wide
To neighbours o'er the fence and 'cross the wall.
There in each place he pauses for a stay
And gets a tasty gift - no small amount
He eats a lot of dinners, eight a day
And breakfasts in the dozens at last count."
"He is a selfish puss to beg and plead!"
"Oh no, he spends his heart and soul to share
And visits only those who're most in need
Of smiling, greeting and of giving care."
"So I don't come here weekly for my tea?"
"You come so love can still be food for me."

A sonnet for the Christmas cats

I wondered if the cats came to the stable
To mew their praises to the Christ-born king
And wind their tails in love around the cradle
Whereon I learned a most satanic thing:
No gospel writes a word on Christmas mogs
In fact of cats the Bible is deprived
While lion, leopard, tigers, gnats and dogs
Chameleons and wolves and quail all thrive.
What story writ of joy won't mention cats?
How holy is a text that has no purrs?
A palimpsest, a shadow-play ersatz!
My godly given reason now demurs:
For those not famed or loved in hallowed way
You are a gift; I praise you; it's your day.

DOGS AND CATS

The more you prance and try
to be her friend

The more you prance and try to be her friend
The hotter burns her hate, full deep your loss
Of status in her eyes, the more your goal
Recedes and you surrender all control
Stop now! No second spent is worth the cost
And will just count against you in the end.
Put hope aside and charm forget. Your role
Is this: in your own company be lost
Curl solo in the sun, to thy will bend
Make I the 1 on whom you can depend
Break trails by moonlight in the winter frost
Split off to find the glue that makes you whole.
Look! Now she comes, purring and at trot
In truth she only wanted what she'd not.

The only time that cat and dog agree

The only time that cat and dog agree
is when my daily dressing I begin.
Eyes wide, they stop and breathless stare at me
perhaps they think I'm taking off my skin.
The cat recoils with sneering whiskered scorn -
"Why bother, fool, you'll never make the mark!"
Kind dog, head cocked, is baffled and concerned -
"Don't change, my lord, you're perfect as you are!"
So easy clothes for you! Your hunting gear,
your bathing suit, pyjamas and sunfrock
are all a onesie cut in finest fur!
Like those of grace who fit where'er they flock:
You gods with beauty born and always dressed
mind us who daily don robes second best.